MW00595420

EP Language Arts 2
Workbook

This book belongs to:

_____

EP Language Arts 2 Workbook

Copyright © 2017   All rights reserved.

This workbook, made by Tina Rutherford with permission from Easy Peasy All-in-One Homeschool, is based on the language arts component of Easy Peasy's curriculum. For EP's online curriculum visit allinonehomeschool.com

Cover design by Yuletide Media – www.yuletidemedia.com

This book may not be reproduced in whole or in part in any manner whatsoever without written permission from Easy Peasy.

ISBN-13: 978-1539168201
ISBN-10: 1539168204

First Edition: January 2017

About this Workbook

This is an offline workbook for Easy Peasy All-in-One Homeschool's Language Arts 2 course. We've modified and expanded upon the online activities and printable worksheets available at the Easy Peasy All-in-One Homeschool website (www.allinonehomeschool.com) so that your child can work offline if desired. Whether you use the online or offline versions, or a combination of both, your child will enjoy these supplements to the Easy Peasy Language Arts course.

How to Use this Workbook

This workbook is designed to be used in conjunction with Easy Peasy's Language Arts 2 Parent's Guide. As you proceed through the Parent's Guide, use this workbook to exercise your child's language arts skills.

This workbook follows the EP online Language Arts course in sequential order, providing 180 daily activity worksheets which can replace online activities and printable worksheets. The daily worksheets are designed with the following guidelines in mind:

- **To supplement daily lessons**
  This workbook on its own supplements, but does not replace, EP's daily lessons. Be sure to check the daily lesson on the website or in the Parent's Guide before having your child do the workbook activities.

- **To serve as an alternative to online activities**
  This workbook serves as an alternative to the activities posted online, providing offline activities in sufficient quantities and varieties to challenge your child. When used in conjunction with the Parent's Guide, this workbook becomes a complete offline course.

Please note, in the various places where nouns and verbs are practiced, certain words can be categorized in more than one place (you can go for a swim [noun] or you can swim [verb]). If your child marks one of them differently than the answer key indicates, have a conversation with them to find out why.

Available Online

- The printable worksheets, a subset of this workbook, are available online.
- The solutions are on the website as well as in the Parent's Guide and are **not included** in this workbook.

Completion Chart for Lessons 1 - 45

#	Topic	#	Topic	#	Topic
1	short a/short i	16	writing/plurals	31	writing
2	writing	17	writing/rhyming	32	writing
3	writing	18	plurals	33	writing
4	writing	19	writing/rhyming	34	writing
5	nouns/capitalization	20	writing/plurals	35	nouns
6	contractions	21	spelling	36	ar sound
7	writing	22	spelling	37	er sound
8	capitalization/ punctuation	23	spelling	38	proper nouns
9	writing/ordering directions	24	spelling	39	spelling - or words
10	capitalization	25	spelling/nouns	40	spelling/nouns
11	compound words	26	writing	41	spelling/proper nouns
12	writing/rhyming	27	writing	42	air sound
13	capitalization/ punctuation	28	singular/plural nouns	43	common/proper nouns
14	writing/rhyming	29	writing	44	oy sound
15	writing/rhyming	30	plural rules	45	ow sound/nouns

Completion Chart for Lessons 46 - 90

#		#		#	
46	aw sound	61	ea words	76	writing
47	al words	62	ou words	77	verbs
48	nouns	63	plural review	78	subject/action and linking verbs
49	story order/long a words	64	oo words	79	verbs
50	ing words	65	ph and gh words	80	writing
51	ink sound/ordering sentences	66	silent letter	81	writing
52	ank sound	67	spelling - oi words	82	verbs
53	noun review/plurals	68	writing	83	action verbs
54	ang sound/story order	69	parts of speech	84	linking verbs
55	ong sound	70	verbs	85	writing/linking verbs
56	ung sound	71	word scramble	86	writing
57	dge sound	72	action verbs	87	writing
58	homonyms	73	plurals	88	writing
59	ey sound	74	action verbs	89	writing
60	le ending	75	writing	90	writing

Completion Chart for Lessons 91-135

91	spelling - oi words	106	spelling	121	spelling
92	linking verbs	107	verb tense	122	possessive nouns
93	linking verbs	108	subjects and verbs	123	possessive nouns
94	linking and action verbs	109	predicates	124	plural possessive nouns
95	ordering directions	110	writing	125	its/it's
96	spelling - aw words	111	spelling	126	spelling
97	past tense/future tense	112	writing/linking verbs	127	its/it's
98	past tense	113	capitalization/ punctuation	128	proofreading
99	ordering sentences	114	contractions	129	verb story
100	writing	115	writing	130	verb story
101	spelling - er words	116	spelling	131	spelling
102	action verbs	117	writing/action verbs	132	short story writing
103	linking verbs	118	capitalization/ punctuation	133	short story writing
104	verb tense	119	ordering directions	134	short story writing
105	writing	120	writing directions	135	short story writing

Completion Chart for Lessons 136-180

136	spelling	151	word match	166	final research project
137	subject pronouns	152	writing	167	final research project
138	object pronouns	153	writing	168	final research project
139	subject and object pronouns	154	writing	169	final research project
140	writing	155	writing	170	final research project
141	word builder	156	writing	171	final research project
142	contractions	157	word builder	172	final research project
143	word match	158	word match	173	final research project
144	nouns/pronouns/verbs	159	writing	174	final research project
145	writing	160	writing	175	final research project
146	blends	161	vowel pairing	176	final research project
147	contractions	162	nouns/verbs	177	final research project
148	spelling suffixes	163	homonyms	178	final research project
149	word builder	164	homonyms	179	final research project
150	writing	165	homonyms	180	verb review

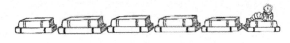

Word Builder

Choose the letters from the word box that best fit the blank within the sentences.
These are short a and short i words.

rip	as	ick	an	ix	lac	ra

Our v___ broke down yesterday.

My dog plays fetch with a st_____.

We had a bl____t at our block party.

I m____ed up a batch of cookie dough.

My favorite dog is a b_____k lab.

We'd love to go to Europe on a t_____ one day.

I had to g____b a cookie before my brother ate them all.

Writing

Describe what tongs look like. Start with "I think tongs look like" and then finish the sentence. Remember to start with a capital letter and end with a period.

_____

_____

_____

_____

_____

_____

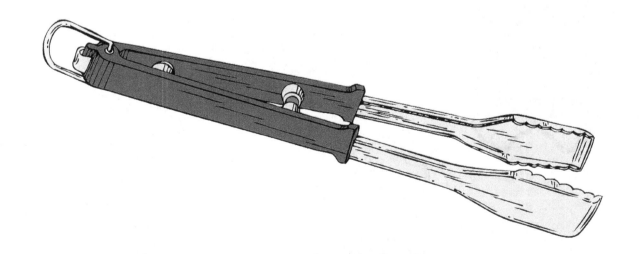

Writing

Write a sentence telling people to be kind to animals. Don't forget a capital letter at the beginning and a period at the end.

_____

_____

_____

_____

_____

Writing

Write a sentence that doesn't make any sense! Here's an example: I drank hamburgers for breakfast. If you need more help you can see the examples at the bottom of the page.

_____

_____

_____

_____

_____

_____

I saw veggies waving as they ran.

A penguin painted my portrait.

The cupcake gave me a balloon.

My flower made a funny face.

Find the Nouns

Color red the common noun flowers. Color blue the proper noun flowers. Names of people, places, and things begin with a capital letter and are proper nouns.

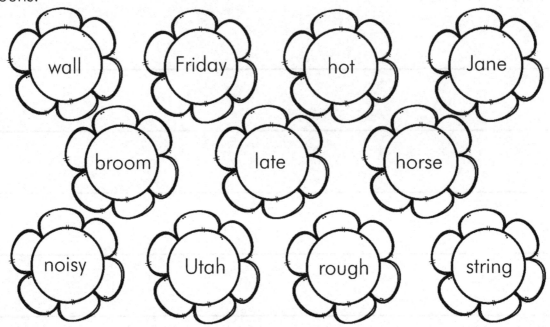

Capitalization

Correct the sentences below by underlining the words that should be capitalized.

what did maria do this morning?

i think i should go to bed early tonight.

can you direct me to memorial hospital?

my brother's name is andy.

i forgot to bring my glasses when we went to ohio.

Contractions

Use this matching game to help you review some contractions and their meanings. First, read through the words – the contraction is to the right of the words it represents. Then cut out the squares, mix them up, flip them over, and try to match them back again.

would not	wouldn't	will not	won't
you have	you've	could not	couldn't
we are	we're	we have	we've
did not	didn't	I will	I'll
can not	can't	she will	she'll

(This page left intentionally blank)

Writing

Write a short story. Here's the beginning: I was pulling weeds in my garden and noticed something unusual sticking up out of the dirt.

_____

_____

_____

_____

_____

_____

_____

_____

_____

_____

Capitalization and Punctuation

Choose the proper way to write each sentence.

a. Jim has a bird   b. jim has a bird?   c. Jim has a bird.   d. Jim has a bird?

a. Howie is a boy   b. Howie is a boy?   c. howie is a boy?   d. Howie is a boy.

a. Pam is sad?   b. Pam is sad   c. Pam is sad.   d. pam is sad.

a. Is Kara home.   b. is Kara home?   c. Is Kara home   d. Is Kara home?

a. are you okay.   b. Are you okay.   c. are you okay?   d. Are you okay?

Write each sentence properly on the line beside it.

jake is two?_____

is maya sick _____

phil is Friendly _____

Writing

Copy these lines of a poem: *The cat she walks on padded claws.*
                                 The wolf on the hills lays stealthy paws.

_____

_____

_____

Ordering Directions

Put these directions for making a peanut butter and jelly sandwich in order using the words in the box.

first	second	third	fourth	fifth	then	finally

_____ Spread the peanut butter
                on the bread.

_____ Put both pieces of
                bread together.

_____ Open the jelly.

_____ Spread the jelly on
                the peanut butter.

_____ Enjoy your lunch!

_____ Open the peanut
                butter.

_____ Gather the bread, peanut
                butter, jelly, and knife.

Correct the Capitalization

Correct the sentences below by underlining the words that should be capitalized. Remember that all sentences must begin with a capital letter. Proper nouns should be capitalized as well. Just do your best and learn from any mistakes!

my favorite holiday is christmas.

my favorite month is december.

my best friend lives on main street.

i like to ride the cable cars in san francisco.

we are going to the zoo on the first friday in april.

she's taking the train to indianapolis next week.

Write the sentences correctly on the lines below them.

i live in the united states.

_____

my dad's name is alan.

_____

Compound Words

A **compound word** is one word made out of two words. *Bedroom* is one word, but it's made from the two words *bed* and *room*. Use the words from the box to make compound words out of the words listed.

| cone | stick | muffs | day | place | ground |
| stairs | ball | shine | boy | cut | chair |

birth_____   wheel_____

cow_____   play_____

up_____   snow_____

sun_____   ear_____

fire_____   pine_____

hair_____   drum_____

Writing

Copy this sentence: *My clothes are soft and warm, fold upon fold, but I'm so sorry for the poor out in the cold.*

_____

_____

_____

_____

_____

Which two words in the sentence above rhyme?

_____   _____

Writing

Copy these lines of a poem: *If all were sun and never rain,*
There'd be no rainbow still.

_____

_____

_____

Capitalization and Punctuation

Underline the words in each sentence that need to be capitalized. Then fill in the
punctuation mark that best fits each sentence.

i'm so excited for thanksgiving

would you like to go to central park

what is your favorite food from taco bell

help

what is your favorite christmas song

my november birthday is on a saturday this year

Writing

Copy this line from a poem by Christina Rossetti: *Stroke a flint, and there is nothing to admire: Strike a flint, and forthwith flash out sparks of fire.*

_____

_____

_____

_____

_____

Which two words in the poem above rhyme?

_____   _____

Writing

Finish this sentence with a rhyme: *If a pig wore a wig,* _____ . What are some words that rhyme with wig? *big, dig, fig, gig, jig...* Here's an example: *If a pig wore a wig, I'd eat a fig*. If you want to, you can draw a picture of your rhyme in the box.

_____

_____

_____

Writing

Copy these two lines of poem by Christina Rossetti:

What will you give me for my pound?
Full twenty shillings round.

_____

_____

_____

Spelling

Remember that **plural** means more than one. Many times a plural word involves an "s" (bikes, toys, balls). Some words don't change form when they are made plural. Copy the word on the line beside it. These are all words that are the same when they are singular (one) or plural (more than one).

deer _____   salmon _____

offspring _____   sheep _____

moose _____   fish _____

Here are two words that are always plural:

scissors _____   pants _____

Writing

Write two lines of a poem like this poem:

What is white? a swan is white
Sailing in the light
What is yellow? pears are yellow,
Rich and ripe and mellow.
What is green? the grass is green,
With small flowers between.

You can use any color you want (blue is easy to rhyme.) If you chose blue, you would start it **What is blue?** Then answer the question and write a rhyme.

_____

_____

_____

_____

Can you think of rhymes for these color words?

pink _____   red _____

black _____   brown _____

white _____   gray _____

Plurals

Choose the correct plural form of the words below.

elf

a. elfs   b. elves

cup

a. cups   b. cupes

patch

a. patches   b. patchs

kiss

a. kiss's   b. kisses

toy

a. toyes   b. toys

baby

a. babys   b. babies

wish

a. wishes   b. wish

fish

a. fishes   b. fish

Fill in the blank with the plural form of the words below.

color _____   box _____

peach _____   play _____

miss _____   berry _____

thief _____   sheep _____

Rhyming

Circle the rhyming words in this poem by Christina Rossetti. Underline the words that repeat.

Fly away, fly away over the sea,
Sun-loving swallow, for summer is done;
Come again, come again, come back to me,
Bringing the summer and bringing the sun.

Write two poem lines. Start each line with a repeating phrase and rhyme the last words. For instance: *Summer's here, summer's here, let's go and <u>play</u>.*
                        Winter's come, winter's come, inside we'll <u>stay</u>.

Make up your own poem or copy the line *Summer's here, summer's here, let's go and play* and then write your own last line. Make sure it rhymes with play!

_____

_____

_____

_____

_____

(This page left intentionally blank)

Writing

Copy the first stanza of this poem by Christina Rossetti.

Boats sail on the rivers,
And ships sail on the seas;
But clouds that sail across the sky
Are prettier far than these.

_____

_____

_____

_____

Here are some plurals that don't follow any rules. Cut them out, mix them up, flip them over, then try to match the word to its plural.

ox	oxen	child	children
woman	women	mice	mouse
person	people	tooth	teeth

(This page left intentionally blank)

Spelling

Write the proper ending on your spelling words.

nd   st

pa ___   sa ___

lo ___   li ___

ne ___   ha ___

gra ___   ca ___

po ___   ru ___

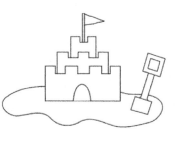

Spelling

Find your spelling words in the wordsearch below. Use the word box if you need to. Then play a game of hangman. The word is in the Parent's Guide.

```
P  A  S  T  K  A  N  T  L
A  H  N  Q  D  Z  A  E  S
M  R  P  W  S  A  N  D  C
U  W  T  A  I  P  W  W  A
L  N  O  Z  L  O  L  Z  S
P  E  P  T  R  N  I  I  T
W  S  R  Y  U  D  S  H  A
H  T  O  H  F  E  T  N  D
R  L  O  S  T  A  L  M  S
A  Q  R  U  S  T  E  V  U
T  Y  P  T  O  H  A  N  D
```

past	nest	list
lost	hand	pond
sand	cast	rust

___ ___ ___ ___ ___

Spelling

Unscramble your spelling words to fill in the blanks.

utrs	nadh	tpsa	slto	scta
ndsa	ndpo	ltsi	sten	drnga

I added milk to the grocery _____.

The birds built a _____ in the tree.

It was _____ noon so we had lunch.

I couldn't find my _____ toy truck.

My sister likes to dig in the _____.

My broken arm is in a _____.

I use my left _____ to write.

We made a _____ entrance.

The ducks swam in the _____.

There was _____ on his bike.

Spelling

Now try to spell your words. Use the pictures to help you remember the words.

My sister likes to dig in the _____.

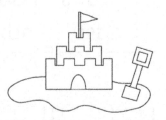

The birds built a _____ in the tree.

My dog's broken leg is in a _____.

I added milk to the grocery _____.

I use my left _____ to write.

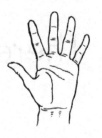

Spelling

Use the lines below to write your spelling words as they are read to you.

_____   _____

_____   _____

_____   _____

_____   _____

_____   _____

Circle the nouns below.

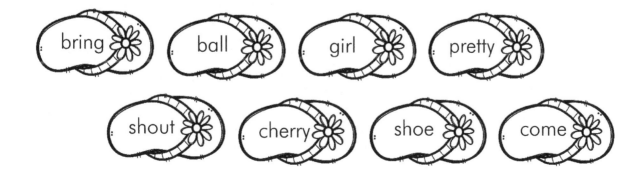

bring   ball   girl   pretty

shout   cherry   shoe   come

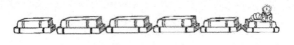

Writing

Copy this sentence: *Now it is a very unusual thing for Mr. Toad to hurry, very unusual indeed.*

_____

_____

_____

Now write a sentence in the same format. Keep the beginning the same, but add in your own word and then tell about it. Then write a comma, "very" and then your word and then "indeed." *It is a very _____ thing _____, very _____ indeed.*

_____

_____

_____

Writing

Copy this sentence: *You know Peter is always ready to go anywhere or do anything that will satisfy his curiosity.*

_____

_____

_____

Now write a sentence in the same format. Copy the sentence below, filling in the blanks as you copy it. *You know _____ is always ready to _____ or do anything that will _____ .*

_____

_____

_____

Singular and Plural nouns

A noun is *singular* when it refers to only one person, place, thing, or idea:

apple   kid   flower   bee

A noun is *plural* when it refers to more than one person, place, thing, or idea:

apples   kids   flowers   bees

The regular plural form of a noun is made by simply adding an **s** to the end of the word. The following list is a mix of singular and plural nouns. If the noun is in the singular form, write its plural form in the blank. If the noun is in the plural form, write its singular form in the blank.

horse _____   balls _____

faces _____   book _____

shirt _____   clock _____

doors _____   game _____

Write four plural nouns from your reading today or another book you've read.

_____ _____ _____ _____

Writing

Copy this sentence: *He envies the birds because they can pour out in beautiful song the joy that is in them.*

_____

_____

_____

Now write a sentence in the same format. Write *Sometimes I envy*, then write a kind of animal, then write **because**, and then write what they can do that you wish you could do.

_____

_____

_____

Plural Rules

The regular plural of nouns is made by adding an S to the end of the word. But there are exceptions to this rule. We call these exceptions **irregular plurals**.

We make the plural of nouns that end in CH, SH, X, or SS by adding ES.

one dress   one fox   one couch
two dresses   two foxes   two couches

We make the plural of some nouns that end in F or FE by changing the F or FE to V and adding ES.

one leaf   one elf
two leaves   two elves

We make the plural of nouns that end in Y not following a vowel by changing the Y to I and adding ES.

one cherry   one fly
two cherries   two flies

And of course, there are many words that just don't follow a rule.

one woman, two women   one child, two children

one sheep, two sheep   one cactus, two cacti

Write the plurals:

knife _____   boy _____

wish _____   miss _____

try _____   man _____

inch _____   hand _____

box _____   girl _____

loaf _____   pie _____

Writing

Copy the sentence below. Make sure you copy the " " (quotation marks) and the ? (question mark).

"What was the use of wasting my breath?" demanded Old Mr. Toad.

_____

_____

_____

Now it's your turn to write a question. Be sure to use a question mark.

_____

_____

_____

Writing

Copy the sentence below. Make sure you copy all of the , (commas) and !
(exclamation points).

Oh, my, no! No indeed!

_____

_____

_____

Now it's your turn to write a sentence of your own that ends in an exclamation
point.

_____

_____

_____

Writing

Copy these sentences. Make sure you copy all of the " (quotation marks) and the ' (apostrophe) and the ? (question mark) and the . (period).

"I'm just watching my babies. Aren't they lovely?" said he.

_____

_____

_____

Now it's your turn to write a sentence of your own that ends in a question mark.

_____

_____

_____

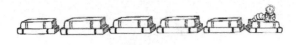

Writing

Copy this sentence. *"Why, I couldn't do that!" he exclaimed right out loud.*

_____

_____

_____

Now it's your turn to write a sentence like the one above. Here's an example: *"I can't believe it!" I shouted.* Write yourself exclaiming something. Use *"* (quotation marks) and ! (exclamation point) and then write who said it. Use the examples. See if you can do it!

_____

_____

_____

Fishing for Nouns

A **noun** is a person (Jeffrey, boy, sister), place (post office, church, Chicago), thing (ball, dog, computer), or idea (love, fear, happiness). Circle the fish below that contain nouns.

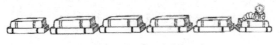

Ar words

Fill in the missing "ar" word using the word box below.

arm	dark	yard	far	barn
car	bark	harp	cart	park

I went out into the _ _ _ _ to play.

We filled our _ _ _ _ at the store.

My dog likes to _ _ _ _ at the TV.

The swings at the _ _ _ _ are fun.

The _ _ _ _ makes a pretty sound.

My grandmother lives _ _ _ away.

The hayloft is in the _ _ _ _.

My sister is afraid of the _ _ _ _.

His _ _ _ was in a sling.

My mom drives a red _ _ _.

Er sound

Fill in the missing "er" word using the word box below. Then write more "er" words on the blank at the bottom.

| serve   skirt   burp   curve   every   blur   turkey   squirrel |

The _ _ _ _ _ _ _ _ ran up the tree.

She had flowers on her _ _ _ _ _.

I _ _ _ _ when I drink soda.

The sign marked the _ _ _ _ _ in the road.

The _ _ _ _ _ _ was delicious.

The cars went so fast they were a

_ _ _ _.

My mother likes to _ _ _ _ _ us dinner.

I brush my teeth _ _ _ _ _ day.

_____

Proper Nouns

Proper nouns are names of people, places, things and ideas. Read the story below. Circle the proper nouns and then write them on the lines below the story. Make sure to capitalize them on the lines!

My favorite day of the week is friday. I start the day with my favorite cereal, choco chunkies. It's a special treat I only get to have on that day. Then I find all of my library books from the previous week. Friday is the day we get to go to central library and pick out new books. I love reading and finding new stories! That afternoon, we get to have lunch at my favorite sandwich shop, anderson's deli. The sandwich I get is called monster cheese. It's so warm and toasty and delicious. That evening is basketball practice. This year, my team is the crushers, and my dad is the coach. I'm on the team with my best friend, james. Finally, when I fall into bed after a long day, it's always nice to realize the next day is saturday, so I can just relax!

1. _____

2. _____

3. _____

4. _____

5. _____

6. _____

7. _____

8. _____

Spelling

Write as many words as you can that have the "or" sound and are spelled with OR. You can use the pictures to help you come up with ideas. Rhyming the words will help you come up with more.

1. _____

2. _____

3. _____

4. _____

5. _____

6. _____

7. _____

8. _____

Spelling

Write these words that make the "i" sound in a different way: *fire, pie, dial, pile, light, bicycle, by, bye, guide*.

_____

_____

_____

A tisket, a tasket, a noun in a basket. Circle the baskets that contain the nouns.

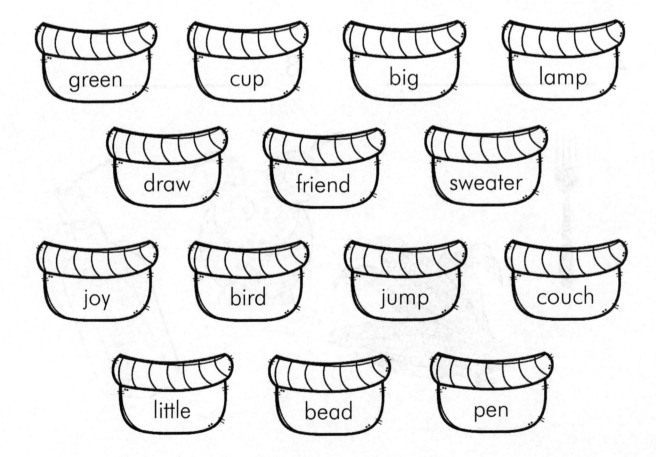

Spelling

Write words that rhyme with bare and are spelled the same way. They should all end in –are. (Here's one to start you off: scare).

1. _____   4. _____

2. _____   5. _____

3. _____   6. _____

Circle the baskets that contain proper nouns.

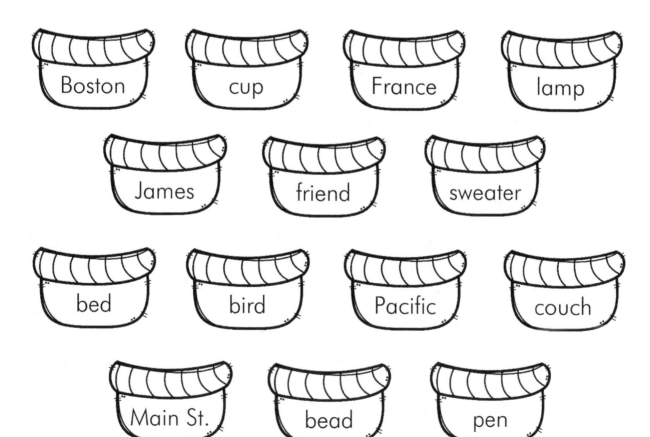

Boston   cup   France   lamp

James   friend   sweater

bed   bird   Pacific   couch

Main St.   bead   pen

Play Ball

Help the basketball player choose the right balls for his game. Color orange the basketballs that have the same vowel sound as . Choose one of the words to write on the blank at the bottom of the page.

floor

fair

mist

trash

hair

trash

cheer

stair

ball

fear

air

_____

Different Nouns

A **noun** is a person, place, thing or idea. A **proper noun** names a *specific* person, place, thing or idea. Since they are names, proper nouns are always capitalized.

Carol   Calvary

A **common noun** is a *general* person, place, thing or idea. Since they are not names, common nouns are only capitalized if they begin a sentence.

girl   church

Are the following nouns common or proper? Write **C** on the lines beside the common nouns and write **P** on the lines beside the proper nouns:

1. cereal _____   6. James _____

2. planet _____   7. Mars _____

3. Mexico_____   8. friend _____

4. chair _____   9. school _____

5. Reno _____   10. zoo _____

Write 3 common nouns: Write 3 proper nouns:

_____   _____

_____   _____

_____   _____

Oy!

Find the hidden toy! Color red all of the spaces with words that have the same vowel sound as "toy." Color the rest of the words brown.

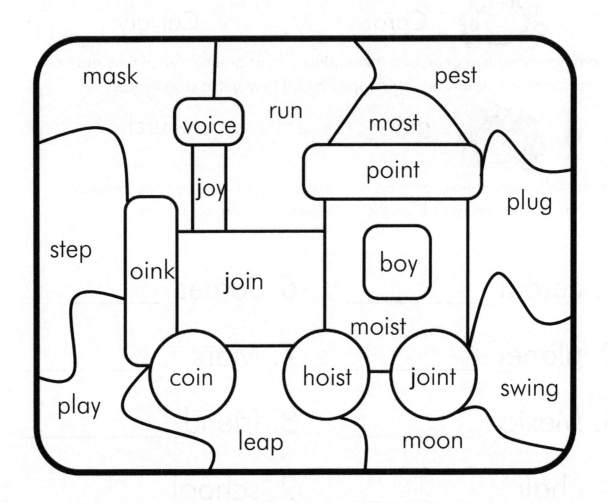

Write your name, phone number, and address:

Name: _____   Phone: _____

Address: _____

Crossword – Ow sound

Fill in the correct word from the word box to complete the crossword puzzle.

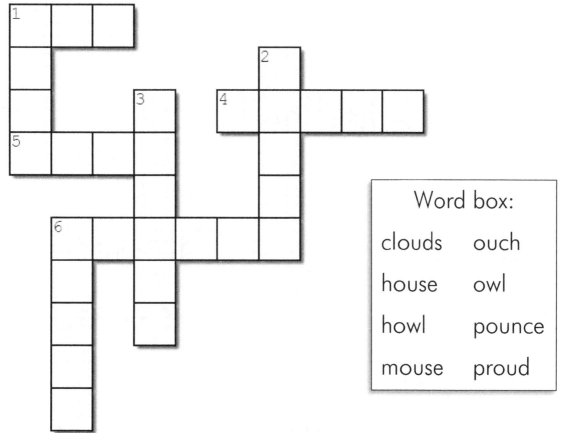

Word box:

clouds	ouch
house	owl
howl	pounce
mouse	proud

Across

1. The _____ was hooting in the trees.
4. The _____ ate all of the cheese.
5. Our dog will sometimes _____ at the door.
6. Some cats love to _____.

Down

1. When I fell off my bike, I screamed, "_____!"
2. Our _____ is the smallest on our street.
3. The sky was full of _____.
6. I am _____ when I work hard.

Circle the common nouns and underline the proper nouns:

cat Utah fast tree big Pete pail face

eat brick Jane meal wall pink Earth

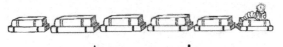

Aw sound

Use the words from the box to fill in the blanks. Then draw a picture of one of the sentences or draw your own "aw" scene.

saw	paw	cause	draw	pause	flaw

My dog licked his _____.

I love to _____ pictures.

We had to _____ the movie.

My biggest _____ is a lack of patience.

I _____ a deer in the backyard.

She's raising money for a good _____.

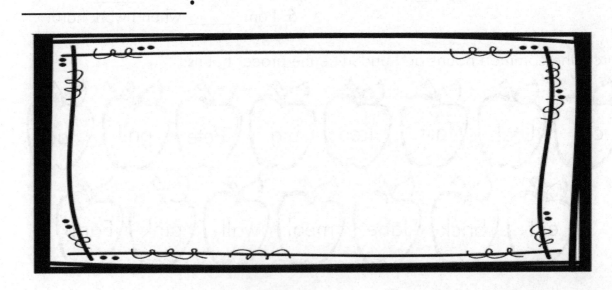

AL words

Use the words from the box to fill in the blanks. Then find them in the word search. Finally, write 3 words that rhyme with the words from the box.

fall	walked	hall	call	all	tall

I heard my mom _____ for me so I _____ down the _____. I tripped over a toy and had quite the _____. I needed a bandage for my knee. Thankfully, I am _____ because they were on the top shelf. As my little sister would say, the bandage made it _____ better.

```
F  A  T  A  L  L  L  C  T  L
A  C  N  Q  D  Z  A  R  A
L  R  G  I  F  T  L  Y  L
L  H  A  L  L  A  L  P  L
B  W  A  L  K  E  D  Z  X
```

_____

Nouns

Circle the common nouns and underline the proper nouns. Then write five common nouns and five proper nouns in the blanks at the bottom.

1. Jessica and Andrew went to Matthew's house.

2. The boys all ran around Northgate Mall.

3. The girls played with the ball at Griffith Park.

4. Maya loved to dress up her doll.

5. Kate had some cake.

6. The book belonged to Jack.

7. Henry was Central Zoo's biggest tortoise.

8. There was a loud noise in the backyard.

Common nouns:

1. _____

2. _____

3. _____

4. _____

5. _____

Proper nouns:

1. _____

2. _____

3. _____

4. _____

5. _____

Story Order

Read the story below. Then put the pictures in the order they happened in the story by numbering the boxes. Finally, underline the 5 words in the story that have the long a sound.

During the week, I do a lot of the same things. I wake up in the morning and make my bed. I have breakfast and then start my school work. I'm usually done by lunch time. After lunch, I love to ride my bike. It's good exercise and a lot of fun. I also like to build things and try to figure out how things work. At the end of a long day, I love to relax in the bathtub. What does your daily schedule look like?

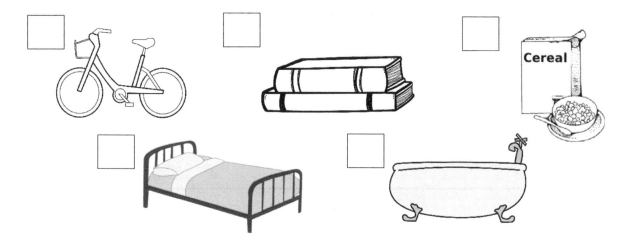

Ing words

Each of the pictures represents a word that ends in **ing**. Write the word beside the picture it represents. Then write four sentences using ing words.

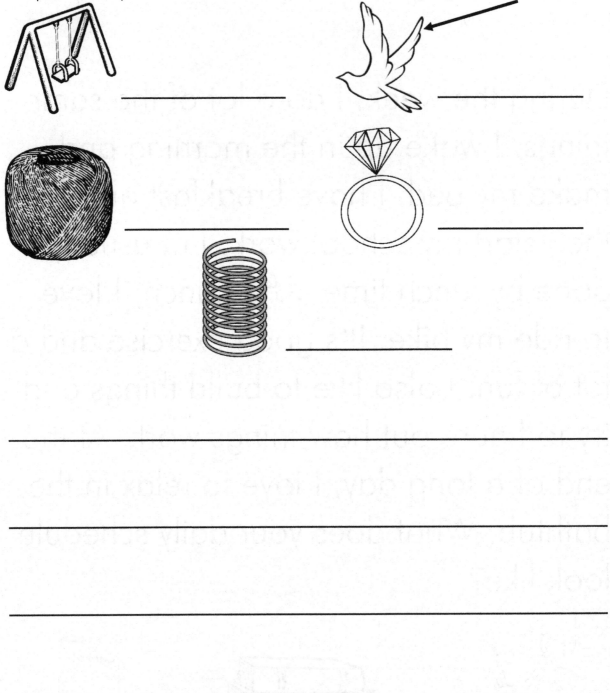

Ink sound

Fill in the blank with the "ink" word from the box that best fits the description.

think	rink	ink	drink	brink	stink	sink
pink	wink	blink	mink			

What a skunk has   _____

When I close my eyes fast   _____

What's inside a pen   _____

What I do with my brain   _____

What I do with milk   _____

Put these sentences in the correct order.

going	park	She	brother.	with	to	her	the	is

_____

_____

coming,	excited!	and	cousin	I'm	is	so	My

_____

_____

Ank sound

Fill in the missing "ank" words below.

| bank | thank | drank | sank | crank | stank | plank | rank |

After the skunk sprayed, the air _____.

I _____ some milk.

My heart _____ when I heard the news.

I always say please and _____ you.

The deck had a loose _____ of wood.

We got some money at the _____.

When I _____ my favorite colors, red is number one.

The old fashioned ice cream maker had a hand _____.

Write a sentence using **smug** or **envious**. Examples: *She thought she was the best swimmer ever and was so* **smug** *about it. She was* **envious** *of how well the other girls could swim.*

_____

_____

Noun Review

Underline all the nouns in each sentence.

The girls played with their dolls in the playroom.

The boys kicked the ball in the backyard.

Samuel read a book in his bed.

The phone rang and woke up Jan.

Write **P** for proper or **C** for common in the blank beside each noun.

book _____   James _____

Chicago_____   sock _____

Jupiter _____   love _____

Write the plural of each word in the blank beside it.

finger _____   cup _____

lamp _____   picture _____

flower _____   friend _____

Write a sentence using **amble** or **hastily**. Examples: *He **ambled** down the street whistling a tune. He **hastily** ate breakfast and spilled his juice.*

_____

_____

Ang sound

Fill in the blanks with the "ang" word that best fits. Then put the pictures in the order of the story by numbering the boxes.

| sang | rang | bang | hang |

The phone _____ and woke me up. It was my Aunt Cathy. She _____ Happy Birthday to me. I sat straight up in bed and tried not to _____ my head on the wall. I told my aunt, "Don't _____ up, but my birthday is next week!" We had a good laugh.

Write a sentence using **indignant** or **scornfully**. Examples: *She was **indignant** that someone would step on her foot. She looked at the bread **scornfully** and said, "I would never eat that!"*

_____

_____

Ong sound

Color orange all of the words in the puzzle that rhyme with "song." Color the rest of the words blue.

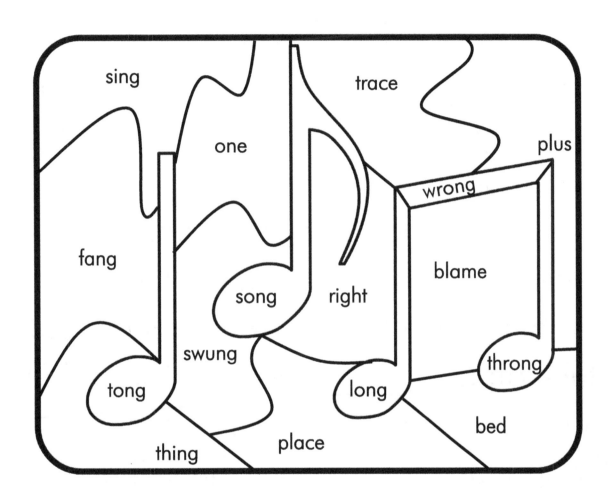

Write a sentence using **anxious** or **feeble**. Examples: *The big storm made him anxious. He has been sick for so long he has become feeble.*

_____

_____

Ung sound

Fill in the "ung" words that best fit the blanks below. Then write 3 more sentences about what the girl does at home.

| sung | rung | hung | swung | flung |

A girl _____ from the monkey bars at the playground. As she _____ there, she thought of the song they had _____ in choir about a monkey swinging through the trees. When she climbed down the ladder, her shoe got stuck on a _____. "Maybe I wouldn't make a very good monkey," she thought as she _____ herself down.

_____

_____

_____

_____

Dge sound

Fill in the "dge" words that best fit the blanks below. One is a proper noun! If you want to, you can color the pictures that correspond to the sentences.

Pledge   edge   badge   fudge   lodge

I earned a _____ in my

scout program.

I love to make peppermint

_____ with my mom.

We stayed at the _____

when we went on vacation.

I saw a rainbow at the

_____ of the clouds.

We said the _____ of

Allegiance.

Write a sentence about anything you want. Remember how to start and finish it.

_____

_____

Homonyms

Homonyms are words that sound alike but have different spellings and meanings. For each sentence below, circle the homonym that best fits the sentence. Learn from any mistakes you make.

The ___ was drinking from the stream.   deer   dear

I ___ the bus and was late.   missed   mist

I really ____ to get more sleep.   knead   need

The ____ flew overhead.   plane   plain

That's my mom over ____.   their   there

The doctor was an ____ late.   our   hour

My cat has a fluffy ____.   tail   tale

The wrong form of the homonym is in each sentence. Circle the incorrect word and write the correct one on the line: **sum**, **rode**, **meat**, and **bear**.

The bare ate all of the honey.   _____

We road our bikes all the way home.   _____

Carnivores eat meet.   _____

Add the numbers to find the some.   _____

Word Scramble

Unscramble the letters to make words that end with the same ending as .

tfyif   _____   50

ydnca   _____

npoy   _____

byab   _____

yenmo   _____

Write a sentence about anything you want. Remember how to start and finish it.

_____

_____

Le ending

Fill in the "le" words that best fit the blanks below. Use the pictures if you need help figuring out the word. You can color the pictures if you want to.

We lit a _____ when the power went out.

My favorite snack is an _____ with peanut butter.

My baby brother loves to drink his _____.

My pet _____ is named Myrtle.

We eat at the dining room _____.

Write a question. What punctuation mark belongs at the end?

_____

_____

Ea words

All of the pencils have "ea" words on them, but they have different sounds! Color red the words that have the same vowel sound as red. Color gray the words that have the same vowel sound as gray.

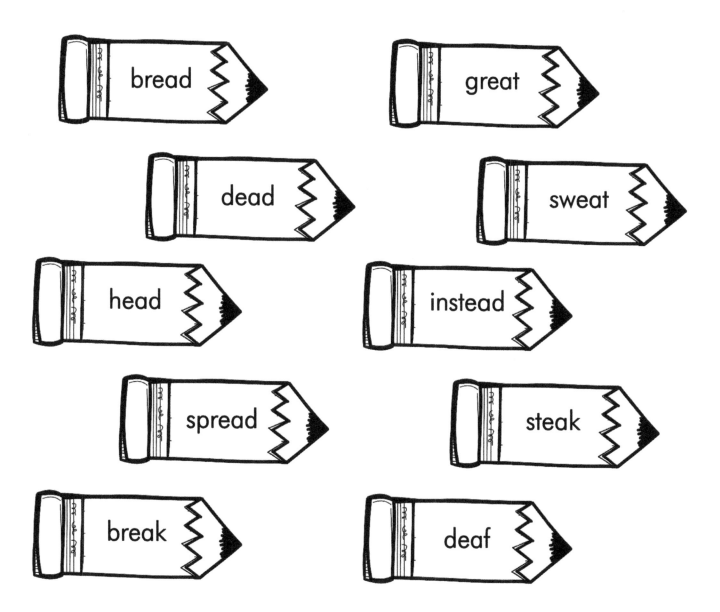

bread

great

dead

sweat

head

instead

spread

steak

break

deaf

How many red pencils are there? _____

How many gray pencils are there? _____

(This page left intentionally blank)

Ou words

Each basket has a word on it. Cut and paste the balloons with the same vowel sound onto the strings coming out of that basket.

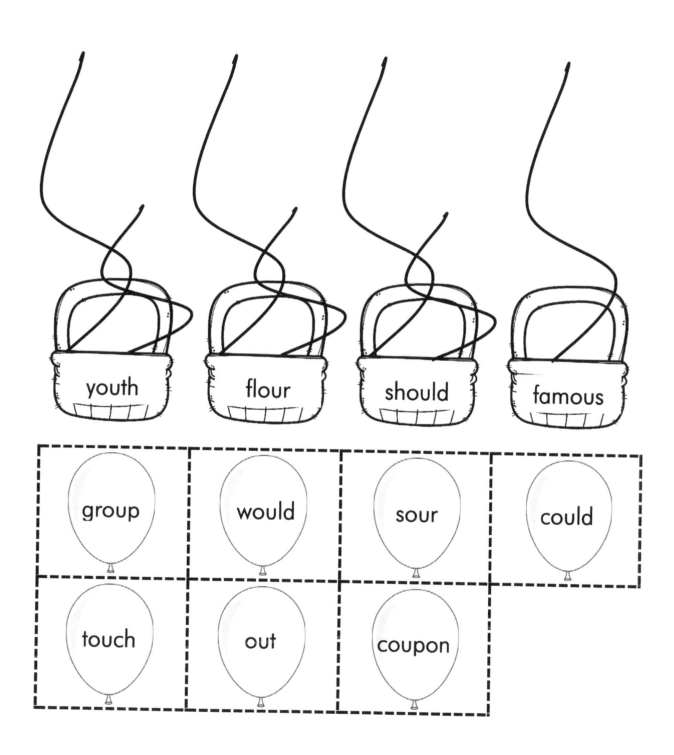

(This page left intentionally blank)

Plural Review

Fill in the plural of each word in the blank beside the word. For many nouns, you simply add an "s" to make it plural. Here are some reminders about the exceptions:

For nouns that end in ch, sh, x, o, or ss, add "es."
For some nouns ending in f or fe, change those endings to "ves."
For nouns that end in a consonant followed by a y, change the y to "ies."
For some nouns that have oo, change oo to "ee."
Many other irregular nouns don't follow any rule: children, deer, men, etc.

foot _____   toy _____

itch _____   elf _____

baby _____   woman_____

fox _____   ball _____

hero _____   deer _____

kiss _____   hug _____

goose_____   knife _____

candy_____   box _____

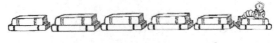

Oo Crossword

Use the pictures to fill in the crossword puzzle. All of the words have "oo" in them.

Across:

2.

4.

5.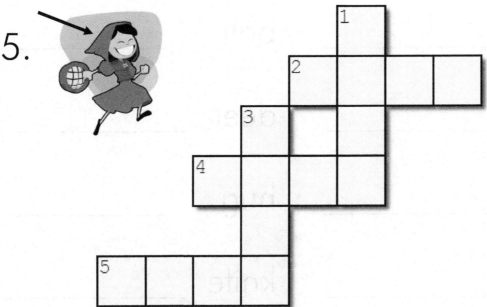

Down:

1.

3.

Writing

Copy this sentence: *He stopped and into his yellow eyes crept a look of suspicion.*

_____

_____

Fill in the blanks with either "gh" or "ph" to make the missing "f" sound. Match the words to the pictures.

___one

___oto

ele___ant

lau___

rou___

Writing

Underline the silent letters in the words that contain them below. Then find those words in the picture. Finally, write them on the lines at the bottom.

two   big   knife   dog   comb   sign   wave   man

_____

_____

Spelling

Copy these words that have the "oi" sound in them: *oil, boil, coin, noise, noisy, avoid, choice, point.*

_____

_____

_____

_____

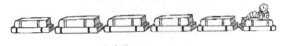

Writing

Write a sentence using at least two words from your spelling list on lesson 67. Here are the words again: *oil, boil, coin, noise, noisy, avoid, choice, point*. Here are examples: *I made the **choice** to **avoid** all **noisy coins**. When **oil boils**, its **noise** is **noisy**.* Make sure your sentences start with a capital letter and end with punctuation!

_____

_____

_____

_____

Writing

Copy this part of a sentence: *Jimmy Skunk was smiling as he ambled towards the old house of Johnny Chuck.* Make sure you make their names start with capital letters. Names are always capitalized.

_____

_____

_____

Parts of Speech

You know that a **noun** is a person, place, thing, or idea. Choose a noun from this list: boy, girl, house, tree, chair.

An **adjective** is a word that describes a noun. Choose an adjective from this list: green, big, striped, happy, tired.

A **verb** is an action word that tells what the noun is doing. Choose a verb from this list: laughing, running, jumping, eating, sleeping.

Now draw a picture that illustrates all three words together.

Verbs

A **verb** is an action word. It tells what the noun is doing. Choose the apple in each row that has the verb. There is one verb in each row.

run   apple   girl

moth   crawl   baby

tree   clock   pillow   hang   breeze

zebra   hair   card   blow   candy

bag   fruit   skip   paper   bike

Spelling

Unscramble the words below. You can use the pictures on the page if you get stuck.

y b b a   _____

g d o   _____

s f i h   _____

a p n   _____

r i g l   _____

d b r i   _____

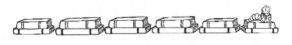

Writing

Try to write this sentence in proper English. Read it out loud to help you figure out what it says: *Ah have mo' important things to worry about.*

_____

_____

_____

Verbs

Remember that verbs show action. Can you find 10 verbs in the words below? Circle them, or color them if you'd like.

Writing

Copy this sentence: *Buster Bear could squash me by just stepping on me, but he doesn't try it.*

_____

_____

_____

_____

Plurals

Write the plural in the blank beside each word.

place _____   tax   _____

match_____   lady   _____

mess _____   wife   _____

Action Verbs

Each line contains one action verb. Circle it.

1. paper   snow   sheet   flying

2. watching   note   brother   bag

3. green   hair   write   cheek

4. cheer   wagon   lamp   tissue

5. chair   sit   tooth   shorts

6. noise   loud   shout   ear

7. library   book   quiet   read

8. giggle   happy   smiley   mouth

9. couch   kneel   shirt   floor

10. ice   water   shoes   type

Writing

Write about your birthday.

_____

_____

_____

_____

_____

_____

_____

_____

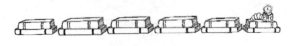

Writing

Write about your favorite thing to do. Why do you like it?

_____

_____

_____

_____

_____

_____

_____

_____

_____

_____

Verb Fishing

Circle or color all of the verb fish below.

Verb Types

Every sentence has a subject (a person or a thing) and a verb. Circle the subject and underline the verb in each of the following sentences.

1. Rebecca painted a beautiful picture.

2. The ball rolled down the hill.

3. I dropped my book.

4. God's creation is magnificent.

5. Mr. Anderson teaches math.

The main verb in a sentence either shows action (**action verbs**) or a state of being (**linking verbs**). Write an A next to the action verbs and an L next to the linking verbs below.

yell _____   are _____

leap _____   want _____

is _____   slept _____

be _____   was _____

Verbs

Remember that verbs show action or a state of being. Circle the verbs in each sentence. Some sentences have more than one!

The phone rang.

The blue van was really loud.

The car raced down the street.

The cat chased after the mouse.

My favorite color is bright green.

There was nothing good on TV.

The cow jumped over the moon.

We were surprised when we heard the news.

The concert was excellent, so I clapped.

Are you circling all of the verbs?

We skipped rope for PE today.

How high can you throw a ball?

They cancelled the class because the speaker was sick.

Writing

Write a short story about what you would do if you saw a skunk. You can start it something like this: "I was taking a walk when all of a sudden a skunk ambled out onto the path in front of me." Then what happened?

_____

_____

_____

_____

_____

_____

_____

_____

_____

Writing

Write a short story about what you would do if you could be invisible.

_____

_____

_____

_____

_____

_____

_____

_____

_____

_____

_____

Find the Verbs

Uncover the hidden picture! If the word is a verb, color the space orange. If it is not a verb, color the space gray.

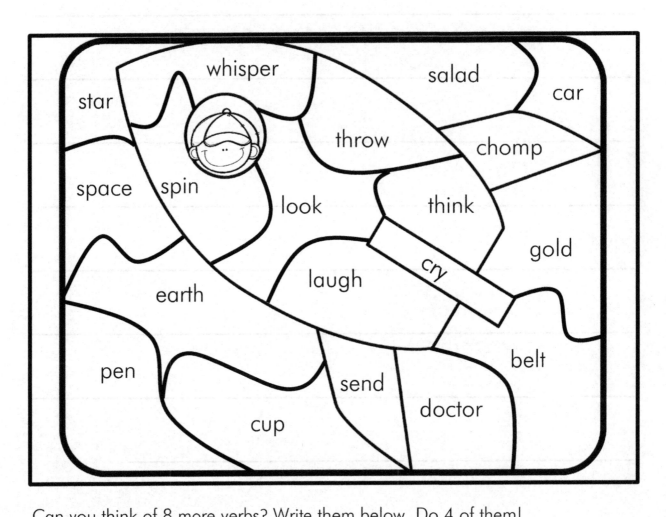

Can you think of 8 more verbs? Write them below. Do 4 of them!

_____   _____

_____   _____

_____   _____

_____   _____

Action Verbs

Remember that action verbs tell what someone or something does. They show action. Circle the action verbs in each of the sentences below.

Show me your picture.

Clean up your room.

Can I come?

He hit the ball.

We honked the horn.

Can we go home?

She ran away.

Play verb charades! Cut or tear a scrap paper into 10 pieces. Write 10 verbs on the pieces. Put them into a bag and take turns with your family drawing a slip of paper and acting out the verb without talking. Try to guess each others' verbs!

To Be

The verb *to be* is a verb that shows a state of being. Use the chart to fill in the missing form of *to be* in each sentence.

Person	Past	Present	Future
I	was	am	will be
you, they, we	were	are	will be
he, she, it	was	is	will be

Uncle Bob _____ home, but now he's not.

The ball _____ flat now since it hit a nail.

Tomorrow it _____ hot.

Yesterday it _____ cold.

I _____ going to the store later.

They _____ loud, but now they _____ quiet.

It _____ a beautiful day, isn't it?

You _____ coming over later.

Writing

Write a sentence that is a question. What punctuation mark should go at the end? Then write an answer that is an exclamation. What punctuation mark should go at the end?

_____

_____

_____

_____

_____

Circle the flowers that contain linking verbs.

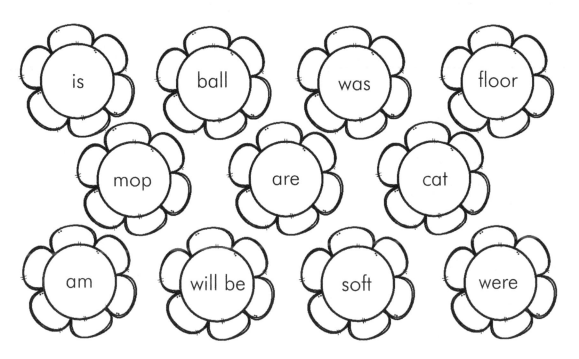

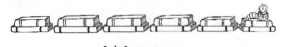

Writing

Put this sentence in order by writing it on the lines. Then write one more sentence in the story. Underline all of the subject nouns and circle all of the predicate verbs. Make sure you write both sentences with a capital letter at the beginning and an end mark at the end. You can use the bottom of the page to draw a picture of your story if you want to.

blue   saw   I   big   a   balloon.

_____

_____

_____

_____

_____

Writing

Put this sentence in order by writing it on the lines. This time, write two more sentences. Underline all of the subject nouns and circle all of the predicate verbs. Make sure you write all sentences with a capital letter at the beginning and an end mark at the end.

circus.   the   family   My   to   went

_____

_____

_____

_____

_____

_____

_____

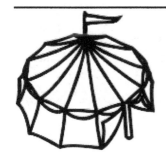

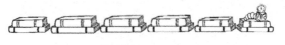
Writing

Put this sentence in order by writing it on the lines. Write two or three more sentences. Underline all of the subject nouns and circle all of the predicate verbs. Make sure you write all sentences with a capital letter at the beginning and an end mark at the end.

the planted She in flowers yard.

_____

_____

_____

_____

_____

_____

_____

Writing

Put this sentence in order by writing it on the lines. Write two or three more sentences. Underline all of the subject nouns and circle all of the predicate verbs. Make sure you write all sentences with a capital letter at the beginning and an end mark at the end.

very   He   his   fast.   drove   car

_____

_____

_____

_____

_____

_____

_____

Writing

Put this sentence in order by writing it on the lines. Write two or three more sentences. Underline all of the subject nouns and circle all of the predicate verbs. Make sure you write all sentences with a capital letter at the beginning and an end mark at the end.

bee searched The flower. for a

_____

_____

_____

_____

_____

_____

_____

Spelling

Find the **oi** words in the puzzle below.

```
W  R  K  K  O  I  L  S  Y  J  P  R  F  T  J
V  P  W  P  B  I  G  E  S  G  Y  J  N  A  M
X  V  B  Q  O  B  W  S  O  I  L  M  Z  B  I
E  S  M  W  I  S  H  E  S  F  U  C  O  L  B
O  M  N  J  N  P  J  O  I  N  T  S  B  E  O
C  F  O  T  G  O  U  E  I  F  Z  P  L  S  I
O  R  I  L  F  I  S  T  O  I  L  B  L  R  L
I  K  S  Y  Y  N  H  K  Y  U  W  N  E  K  L
L  N  E  S  F  T  J  O  I  N  W  L  A  W  Z
E  I  E  T  X  L  L  N  S  A  O  S  V  K  B
V  V  S  M  O  W  V  S  X  I  Y  J  E  D  A
H  E  Y  B  F  D  E  O  E  C  Z  D  S  D  B
U  S  F  O  I  L  S  G  R  O  V  N  Y  N  I
I  A  J  V  J  F  I  G  C  I  I  X  Q  H  E
W  Q  E  V  L  I  A  B  I  N  E  S  Y  W  S
```

oil	join	foil
boil	coin	toil
coil	joint	boing
soil	point	noise

(continued on next page)

Spelling

Practice spelling your words! Have someone read you the words from the previous page and try to write them from memory onto the lines below.

_____   _____

_____   _____

_____   _____

_____   _____

_____   _____

_____   _____

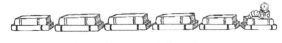

Linking Verbs

Circle the linking verbs in the sentences below.

The boy was happy.

August will be hot.

The grapes look delicious.

Babies are cuddly.

The butterfly is beautiful.

My dog seems hyper.

Basketball is my favorite sport.

Now write two sentences with linking verbs on the lines below.

_____

_____

_____

_____

Linking Verbs

Circle the linking verbs in the sentences below. Some of them aren't in the "to be" form. One sentence has an action verb in it. Can you find it? Underline it.

My dad is an architect.

The mail will be delayed tomorrow.

The girls were tired after their soccer game.

The girl seems shy.

I went to the store yesterday.

It was very windy today.

My dog looks hungry.

Your turn! Write two sentences with linking verbs. Circle your linking verbs.

_____

_____

_____

_____

Verbs

Find and write five linking verbs and five action verbs from something you've read recently. Remember, every sentence has a verb!

Linking Verbs

_____

_____

_____

_____

_____

Action Verbs

_____

_____

_____

_____

_____

Ordering Directions

Put these directions for making a pizza in order using the words in the box.

| first | second | third | fourth | fifth | then | finally |

_____ Spread the crust out on the pan.

_____ Put the pizza in the oven.

_____ Spread tomato sauce on the crust.

_____ Remove from oven and cut.

_____ Enjoy your pizza!

_____ Add toppings and cheese.

_____ Gather the ingredients.

Spelling

Find the **aw** words in the puzzle below.

```
W R K C L A W S Y J P R F T J
V P W P S I G E S G Y J N A M
X V B Q T B W F L A W M Z B I
E S M W R S H E S F U C O L P
O M P J A Y D R A W T S B E A
J F A T W A U E I F Z P L S W
A R W L F W S L A W N B L R N
W K S Y Y H K Y U W N E K L
L N E S F T L A W D W L A W Z
E I E T X L L N S A O S V K B
V V S M O W V S X D Y J E D A
H E Y B F D E O E R Z D S D B
U S R A W L S G R A V N Y N I
I A J V J F I G C W I X Q H E
W Q E V L I A B I N E S Y W S
```

claw	jaw	pawn
flaw	paw	law
straw	yawn	raw
draw	lawn	drawn

(continued on next page)

Spelling

Practice spelling your words! Have someone read you the words from the previous page and try to write them from memory onto the lines below.

_____   _____

_____   _____

_____   _____

_____   _____

_____   _____

_____   _____

Matching

Cut out the squares, mix them up and lay them face down on the table. Play a matching game where you match the sentences to either the **past tense** (already happened) or **future tense** (will happen later) of the verb in parentheses at the bottom.

We ___ cards last night. **(play)**	**played**	We ___ golf next week. **(play)**	**will play**
We ___ up the answer when we weren't sure. **(look)**	**looked**	Later tonight we ___ at the stars. **(look)**	**will look**
Last Christmas I ___ most of my relatives. **(see)**	**saw**	We ___ the new movie when it comes out. **(see)**	**will see**

Copy this sentence: *"The bride looked like a queen."* Do you think that's a nice way to describe her? Is it better than saying she looked pretty? What image do you picture?

_____

_____

(This page left intentionally blank)

Past Tense

Verbs in the **past tense** are showing that something already happened. To make most verbs past tense, you simply add "ed" to the end. There are some exceptions to this. Read the examples and then make the verbs past tense.

If a verb ends in e, simply add "d" instead of "ed" (bake = baked).

race _____   please _____

tame _____   fake _____

If a verb ends in a consonant followed by a y, change the y to an i and then add "ed." If it ends in a vowel followed by a y, leave the y and add "ed." This is similar to the plural rule for words ending in y (carry = carried, play = played).

hurry _____   obey _____

cry _____   stay _____

Make these verbs past tense.

place _____   jump _____

dry _____   wash _____

color _____   clean _____

enjoy _____   ask _____

like _____   try _____

guess _____   worry _____

Ordering Sentences

Put these words in the order that makes a complete sentence. Add proper punctuation.

makes   Jane   dinner

_____

laundry   folded   Mom

_____

will order   We   pizza

_____

Pick the answer that best fits the sentence. Remember that each sentence needs a subject noun and predicate verb.

The dog _____.
a. bone
b. dug a hole
c. leash

The ball _____.
a. bouncy
b. green
c. rolled

_____ flew in a line.
a. Wing
b. Run
c. The birds

_____ was tasty.
a. Eat
b. The drink
c. Jump

Writing

Write about what you did yesterday. Use the words **first**, **next**, and **last** to start your sentences. That means your story should be in order. What did you do first? What did you do next? What did you do last? Write at least three sentences, starting each one with one of those words.

_____

_____

_____

_____

_____

_____

_____

Writing

Copy this sentence: *"But why do you carry that door?" asked the sheriff.* Make sure you write all of the punctuation. There are quotation marks showing that someone is speaking. There is a question mark showing that he is asking a question. There is a period to end the sentence. Also watch your spelling.

_____

_____

Spelling

Find the **er** words in the puzzle below.

```
H  E  R  D  L  A  W  S  Y  B  P  R  F  T  J
V  M  I  S  T  E  R  E  S  L  Y  J  N  A  T
H  V  B  Q  T  B  W  S  L  I  W  M  Z  B  I
E  S  I  S  T  E  R  I  C  S  U  O  O  L  S
R  M  P  J  A  Y  D  L  A  T  W  T  F  E  T
B  F  A  T  W  A  U  V  I  E  Z  H  E  S  E
A  R  W  L  F  W  S  E  A  R  N  E  R  L  R
V  E  R  B  Y  N  H  R  Y  U  W  R  N  K  N
B  E  F  F  A  T  H  E  R  P  D  Z  H  E  R
```

her	stern	mister
verb	fern	blister
silver	herb	mother
sister	herd	father

(continued on next page)

Spelling

Practice spelling your words! Have someone read you the words from the previous page and try to write them from memory onto the lines below.

_____   _____

_____   _____

_____   _____

_____   _____

_____   _____

_____   _____

Action Verbs

For each sentence, find the action verb and write it in the blank.

We went to the store early Friday morning. _____

We put the groceries into the shopping cart. _____

We had to wait at the checkout for a long time. _____

We finally paid the cashier for our groceries. _____

We then loaded our car with all of the groceries. _____

We carefully drove home for a late lunch. _____

Which word is the action verb in each sentence?

I read the whole book.

a. read   c. whole

b. book   d. the

My dad grilled our burgers.

a. dad   c. burgers

b. my   d. grilled

She sat on the cold bench.

a. cold   c. sat

b. bench   d. on

We went to the beach.

a. beach   c. to

b. went   d. we

The bag hung on the hook.

a. hook   c. hung

b. bag   d. on

The ice cracked in the glass.

a. cracked   c. in

b. ice   d. glass

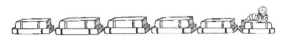

Linking Verbs

For each sentence, find the linking verb and write it in the blank.

That girl seems nice and friendly to me. _____

All the kids who came look so happy. _____

She was so hungry she wanted seconds. _____

Harold is an award-winning sushi chef. _____

Her shoes are the muddiest I've ever seen. _____

My dad is thirsty and is asking for iced tea. _____

Which word is the verb in each sentence?

We were late for church.

a. late   c. church
b. we   d. were

My sister has been sick.

a. My   c. has been
b. sister   d. sick

The baby is hungry.

a. the   c. is
b. baby   d. hungry

She feels very cold.

a. She   c. very
b. feels   d. cold

His room was a mess.

a. his   c. mess
b. was   d. room

They will be here tomorrow.

a. tomorrow   c. will be
b. here   d. they

Verb Tense

The verb tense places a verb in time. The three main tenses are **past tense** (already happened), **present tense** (happening right now), and **future tense** (will happen later). Use the chart to help you fill in the right verb for each sentence. If you're having trouble, read the sentence out loud with each choice. The one that sounds right is probably the right one. Put a star next to the sentence in **present tense**.

Past	Present	Future
I baked cupcakes.	I bake cupcakes.	I will bake cupcakes.
I was baking cupcakes.	I am baking cupcakes.	I will be baking cupcakes.
I had been baking cupcakes.	I have been baking cupcakes.	I am going to bake cupcakes.

We _____ to church tomorrow.
(went/will go)

I _____ my bike yesterday.
(rode/ride)

My sister _____ right now.
(slept/is sleeping)

Yesterday, we _____ pancakes.
(eat/ate)

I _____ God forever.
(followed/will follow)

Writing

Choose three action verbs. They can be any three action verbs you want. Write them in the blanks:

_____   _____   _____

Now write three sentences using your three verbs. Make sure the sentences and the verb tense match!

_____

_____

_____

_____

_____

_____

_____

_____

Spelling

Put an X over the cloud in each row that contains the misspelled word.

went   luv   night

lik   self   dog

bird   babys   yard

horse   corn   gote

lift   cart   moov

push   giv   get

Verb Tense

Write the correct tense of the action verb to match the rest of the sentence.

(to dig) Yesterday, my dog _____ a hole.

(to sing) I _____ a solo next week.

(to write) I _____ a poem last night.

(to sleep) She _____ right now.

(to play) Later, we _____ outside.

(to cook) Whenever he _____, I eat well.

(to watch) We _____ the game now.

(to run) I _____ a race last week.

(to eat) I _____ too much earlier.

(to sit) Next time, I _____ beside you.

(to kick) Watch! She _____ the ball hard.

(to fly) That bird always _____ at night.

Writing

Copy any sentence from a book you are reading. What is the subject? What did the subject do (what is the predicate)? Make sure to start your sentence with a capital letter and end it with punctuation.

_____

_____

_____

Subjects and Verbs

Circle the subject and underline the verbs in the sentences below.

After breakfast, Justin cleaned the table.

The shy little girl hugged her mom's leg.

The hyper puppy dropped his ball at my feet.

The food was piping hot.

Sandra forgot her flute for band rehearsal.

William ran the ball up the field.

Predicates

The complete **predicate** is anything that isn't the subject – it tells what the subject of the sentence does. Underline the complete predicate in each sentence below.

Riley swept the kitchen.

Andrew rode his bike.

Olivia threw the ball.

The surfer caught the big wave.

The phone rang loudly.

The pig rolled in the mud.

The rainbow appeared over the clouds.

The dishwasher cleaned the dishes.

My mom went to the store.

Writing

There's a story where the ruler, a tyrant, made a law that everyone had to bow down to his hat. Pretend that you are king of a country. Write about what laws you would make.

_____

_____

_____

_____

_____

_____

_____

_____

Spelling

Copy each of the words onto the line beside it. Be sure to spell each word correctly!

bright _____   pull _____

eat _____   push _____

far _____   right _____

fight _____   seen _____

flight _____   sight _____

lost _____   strength_____

might _____   tight _____

pole _____   wire _____

Writing

Copy this sentence. It's a little tricky! *"The man who has made up his mind to win,"* said Napoleon, *"will never say impossible."* Be careful to use commas and quotation marks to show someone is speaking. There are also two capital letters in this sentence.

_____

_____

_____

_____

Linking Verbs

Circle the linking verbs below.

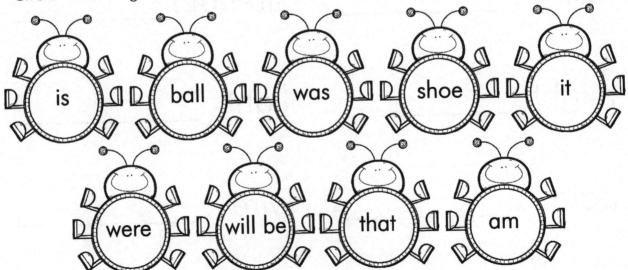

Capitalization and Punctuation

Correct the sentences by underlining the words that should be capitalized and adding any missing punctuation.

my dog is so silly when he chases his tail

mr. robinson was my favorite teacher.

have you ever been to another country

watch out for that patch of ice

we went to alabama last tuesday.

Writing

Copy this sentence. *At first the Romans, who were very proud and brave, did not think there was much danger.* Make sure you use two capital letters and two commas.

_____

_____

_____

_____

Contractions

In the first section, choose the correct meaning of the contraction. In the second section, write the correct meaning of the contraction. In the last section, try to write the correct contraction for the words given.

we'll
a. they will   c. will not
b. we will   d. we are

haven't
a. do not   c. has not
b. will not   d. have not

you're
a. I am   c. you are
b. I will   d. you have

I've
a. I have   c. could have
b. we have   d. have not

I'll _____   we've _____

he'll _____   don't _____

didn't _____   aren't _____

I'm _____   you'll _____

were not _____

should have _____

Writing

Write a story about the time you ran into a lion.

_____

_____

_____

_____

_____

_____

_____

_____

_____

Spelling

Look at each word, then cover it and try to write it on your own onto the line beside it. Check your spelling and correct any mistakes. These are the same words from lesson 111. Do you remember them?

bright _____   pull _____

eat _____   push _____

far _____   right _____

fight _____   seen _____

flight _____   sight _____

lost _____   strength_____

might_____   tight _____

pole _____   wire _____

Writing

Copy this sentence. *Nearly two thousand years ago there lived in Rome a man whose name was Julius Caesar.* Make sure you use capital letters in the right place and make sure you spell his name correctly.

_____

_____

_____

_____

Action Verbs

Circle the action verbs below.

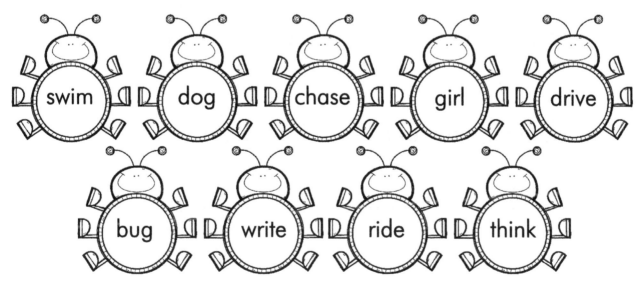

Capitalization and Punctuation

Underline the words that need to be capitalized and add the missing punctuation. For the final sentence, rewrite it correctly on the lines.

the teacher's name was mr. king

i asked michelle to come with me to chicago

why is it so cold today

my favorite park is central park

we went to new york last week and it was so crowded

are you going to metropolis zoo with us on friday

watch out for that angry dog

aunt cathy and i are going christmas shopping

can you help me make lunch for timothy

_____

_____

Ordering Directions

Put these directions for making a snowman in order using the words in the box.

first   second   third   then   finally

_____ Stack the three balls largest to smallest.

_____ Make the next ball slightly smaller.

_____ Roll a large ball for the base of your snowman.

_____ Add eyes, nose, mouth, and arms.

_____ Make the last ball the smallest of all.

Put these directions for making scrambled eggs in order using the words in the box.

first   second   third   fourth   fifth   then   finally

_____ Whisk the cracked eggs and milk in the bowl.

_____ Cook over medium heat until done.

_____ Serve with toast and enjoy!

_____ Crack the eggs into the bowl.

_____ Pour a splash of milk into the bowl of eggs.

_____ Pour the whisked eggs into the pan.

_____ Gather the eggs, whisk, milk, bowl, and pan.

Writing Directions

Most of the directions for making a milkshake are written for you. However, the time words (for example: **first, second, next, then, after that, finally, last**) are missing. Fill in the blank beside each step with a time word that makes sense for that step of the directions. Be sure to capitalize it. There are many right answers.

_____, get out the blender and plug it in.

_____, get out the ice cream, milk, and any toppings you want to add.

_____, scoop the ice cream, pour the milk, and dump any toppings into the blender.

_____, put the lid on the blender and mix until everything is well blended.

_____, pour into a glass and enjoy!

Spelling

Copy each of the words onto the line beside it. Be sure to spell each word correctly!

answer_____   model_____

classify_____   paragraph_____

cough_____   rough _____

dough_____   store _____

enough_____   though_____

glyph _____   tough _____

graph _____   triumph_____

laugh _____   wide _____

Writing

Write the name: **Alexander the Great.**

_____

Possessive Nouns

Choose the noun that shows possession. Things like the dog's bone, the house's door, the girl's hair – these all show possession. Notice the 's? Circle the choice that best fits in the blank.

The _____ melody was catchy.
   songs'   song's

The _____ voice was scratchy.
   boy's   boys'

The _____ tire was flat.
   bike's   bikes'

The _____ claws were sharp.
   cats'   cat's

My _____ pages are worn.
   books'   book's

Possessive Nouns

Circle the choice that best fits the blank.

The _____ frosting was delicious.
   cupcakes'   cupcake's

The _____ sail was colorful.
   boat's   boats'

The _____ laugh was adorable.
   baby's   babies'

Writing

Write the name of five people in your family. Now make them each own something by adding 's. For example: *Mom's computer*.

_____

_____

_____

_____

Plural Possessive Nouns

When a noun is plural or ends in an s and you want to make it possessive, in most cases you add the apostrophe after the s like this **s'**. For example Jame**s'** shirt, the girl**s'** dresses (this is more than one girl), the boy**s'** games (this is more than one boy). Circle the correct answer for each sentence. Is it plural? Is it possessive?

The three _____ clothes matched.
    girls'   girl's

The two _____ stars were red.
    balls'   ball's

Her _____ names were Rex and Max.
    dog's   dogs'

The seven _____ backs were gray.
    chair's   chairs'

_____ car was red.
    James'   Jame's

Writing

Write this: *Genghis Khan's hawk.*

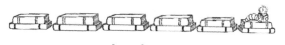

Its/It's

When **it** is possessive, you do not use an apostrophe. When you use an apostrophe in the word, you turn it into a contraction that means "it is." Circle the form of **it** that best fits each sentence. Then write two sentences at the bottom. One should use *its* and mean that something belongs to it. The other should use *it's* and mean it is.

The dog got _____ fur muddy.
    its   it's

_____ really hot outside today.
 Its   It's

I think _____ fun to play in the rain.
    its   it's

_____ house is a hole in the wall.
 Its   It's

_____

_____

_____

Spelling

Look at each word, then cover it and try to write it on your own onto the line beside it. Check your spelling and correct any mistakes. These are the words from lesson 121. Do you remember them?

answer_____   model_____

classify_____   paragraph_____

cough_____   rough _____

dough_____   store _____

enough_____   though_____

glyph _____   tough _____

graph _____   triumph_____

laugh _____   wide _____

Its/It's

Circle the form of **it** that best fits each sentence. Then write two new sentences at the bottom. One should use *its* and mean that something belongs to it. The other should use *it's* and mean it is.

It was so old _____ paint was flaking off.

    its   it's

_____ a beautiful rainbow!

    Its   It's

That's a pretty color. What is _____ name?

    its   it's

_____ Friday today.

    Its   It's

_____

_____

_____

_____

Proofreading

Correct the sentences! The mistakes have been underlined. Do you know how to correct them? Write the corrected sentence on the lines.

My aunt, uncle, <u>en</u> cousins <u>is</u> visiting today_

_____

_____

They always <u>brings</u> <u>they're</u> dogs_

_____

_____

<u>the</u> <u>dog's</u> names are <u>max</u> and <u>titan</u>.

_____

_____

Do you have a fun <u>ant</u> <u>en</u> uncle, too<u>.</u>

_____

_____

Crazy Story

Fill in the blanks with the action verb requested without looking at the story. Then use the numbers to fill out the crazy story. Read it to someone else.

1. -ing verb _____

2. past tense verb _____

3. past tense verb _____

4. past tense verb _____

5. past tense verb _____

6. -ing verb _____

7. present tense verb _____

8. present tense verb _____

9. past tense verb _____

10. present tense verb _____

I had a weird dream that my sister was __1__ in the bathtub. She __2__ and __3__ until finally she _4_. I __5__ my favorite stuffed animal and was __6__ to get her when I woke up. I felt like I wanted to __7__ and __8__, but instead I __9__ to __10__ her. She thought I was crazy.

Crazy Story

Fill in the blanks with the action verb requested without looking at the story.
Then use the numbers to fill out the crazy story. Read it to someone else.

1. past tense verb _____

2. past tense verb _____

3. present tense verb _____

4. past tense verb _____

5. past tense verb _____

6. -ing verb _____

7. past tense verb _____

8. past tense verb _____

9. -ing verb _____

10. past tense verb _____

I went to the store with my mom. She __1__ a cart and
we __2__ shopping. I was going to __3__ something
off the shelf, but it __4__ on my head. I __5__ it into
the cart and was __6__ to catch up with my mom
when I __7__ my best friend. We ____8____ for a
minute, but I knew my mom was __9__ so I __10__ .

Spelling

Copy each of the words onto the line beside it. Be sure to spell each word correctly!

addition_____   glass_____

confusion_____   key_____

direction _____   location_____

division_____   recreation_____

education_____   sensible_____

explosion_____   subtraction_____

fiction_____   support_____

fig _____   vacation_____

Writing

You are going to write a short story, one sentence at a time. Today, write one sentence with a subject and a predicate. Here are some examples:

I ran home.

My dog ate all the crumbs from around the table.

Someday I'm going to fly away in a hot air balloon.

_____

_____

_____

Writing

Add another sentence to the one you wrote on lesson 132. Just write your new sentence below but make sure it goes with the one you already wrote. In this sentence, use an apostrophe. Here are examples:

I ran home. My sister**'s** bike was lying in the driveway.

My dog ate all the crumbs from around the table. He found the most underneath my brother**'s** high chair.

Someday I'm going to fly away in a hot air balloon. The balloon**'s** name is going to be the *Explorer*.

_____

_____

_____

Writing

Add another sentence to the one you wrote on lesson 133. Just write your new sentence below but make sure it goes with the one you already wrote. Here are examples:

I ran home. My sister's bike was lying in the driveway. I thought I'd take it for a spin.

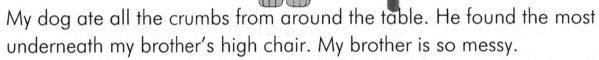

My dog ate all the crumbs from around the table. He found the most underneath my brother's high chair. My brother is so messy.

Someday I'm going to fly away in a hot air balloon. The balloon's name is going to be the *Explorer*. I think I'll fly it to Africa.

_____

_____

_____

Writing

Add another sentence to the one you wrote on lesson 134. This time you will connect it to the sentence you wrote before using **and**, **but**, or **or**. Take away the punctuation mark from the end of your sentence and write a comma instead. Then write **and**, **but**, or **or** and then your new sentence. Here are examples:

I ran home. My sister's bike was lying in the driveway. I thought I'd take it for a spin, **but** just then she came out of the house and said she was going to ride it.

My dog ate all the crumbs from around the table. He found the most underneath my brother's high chair. My brother is so messy, **and** he loves to throw his food on the floor.

Someday I'm going to fly away in a hot air balloon. The balloon's name is going to be the *Explorer*. I think I'll fly it to Africa, **or** maybe I'll float to Asia.

_____

_____

_____

_____

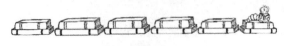

Spelling

Look at each word, then cover it and try to write it on your own onto the line beside it. Check your spelling and correct any mistakes. These are words from lesson 131. Do you remember them?

addition_____   glass_____

confusion_____   key_____

direction _____   location_____

division_____   recreation_____

education_____   sensible_____

explosion_____   subtraction_____

fiction _____   support_____

fig _____   vacation_____

Subject Pronouns

Use the chart below to fill in the missing subject pronouns from the sentences.
(You probably don't even need the chart, but it's there if you do!)

Person	Singular	Plural
1st (speaking)	I	we
2nd (spoken to)	you	you
3rd (spoken about)	he/she/it	they

(Meg, Jill, and I) _____ played ball together.

(Your dad) _____ works hard at his job.

([Speaking to] Tom) _____ are being too loud.

(The dog and cat) _____ chased each other.

(Philadelphia) _____ is a city rich in history.

(You and I) _____ are on the same team.

(Jack and Tom) _____ are on the other team.

(My Aunt Sally) _____ is a nurse.

(The apple) _____ was sweet.

(My brother) _____ likes sweet apples.

Object Pronouns

Use the chart below to fill in the missing object pronouns from the sentences.
(You probably don't even need the chart, but it's there if you do!)

Person	Singular	Plural
1st (speaking)	me	us
2nd (spoken to)	you	you
3rd (spoken about)	him/her/it	them

Brian wanted to play with_____. (Meg, Jill, and me)

You must really love _____. (Your dad)

I am talking to _____. ([Speaking to] Tom)

I tried to keep up with _____. (The dog and cat)

Last year, we visited _____. (Philadelphia)

The coach seems to like _____. (You and me)

I hope we don't lose to _____. (Jack and Tom)

The other nurses really like _____. (My Aunt Sally)

The orange wasn't sweet like _____. (The apple)

Apples taste better to _____. (My brother)

Subject and Object Pronouns

Is the missing pronoun a subject or an object pronoun? Write the correct form of the pronoun in the blank.

I wanted to play with_____, but she was busy.
                          she/her

You must really love your dad. _____ works hard.
                                He/Him

I tried to keep up with _____, but they kept running.
                        they/them

You and I will have fun if the coach puts _____ in.
                                          we/us

Jack and Tom are good. _____ will be hard to beat.
                        They/Them

My Aunt Sally is kind, so the other nurses like _____.
                                                she/her

My Aunt Sally thinks _____ are kind too.
                     they/them

My mom went to the store. _____ forgot her list.
                          She/Her

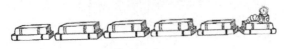

Writing

Write a sentence with someone's name in it. For example: *Samuel likes to climb walls*. Write a second sentence with a pronoun instead of the name. For example: *He can literally climb up and touch the ceiling*. Now write one last sentence. Use an apostrophe with the name, either showing possession or being used as a contraction. For example: *Samuel's really amazing!* (Samuel is really amazing) or *Samuel's feet are strong to hold him up so high.* (The feet belong to Samuel.) You should have three sentences.

_____

_____

_____

_____

_____

_____

_____

Word Builder

Choose the letters from the box that best fit the blanks within the sentences. Write them in your neatest handwriting. Write each completed word again on the lines at the bottom of the page.

| co | ag | ace | it | gy | oal |

I scored a g_____ in last week's soccer game.

I don't mean to br_____, but my mom is the best!

Our c_____y got a new mayor.

The _____t was hard and cold.

The look on her f_____ was happy.

My dad and I went to the _____m to shoot some hoops.

_____

_____

Contractions

Find which tree the contraction apple goes to. Draw a line from the apple to the right tree. Then write all of the contractions in your best handwriting on the lines at the bottom.

_____

_____

_____

Word Match

Draw a line from the word to its definition. Then write all of the words on the lines at the bottom, using your very best handwriting.

attention

dough

recipe

bakery

ingredients

larvae

officer

customer

customs

baby insects that look like tiny worms

a person who buys things

a mixture of ingredients used to make bread, cookies, and more

the parts that make up a mixture

things members of a group usually do similarly

a store that makes and sells things like bread and cake

directions used for cooking

looking and listening carefully

a person who enforces laws

_____

_____

_____

Nouns, Pronouns, and Verbs

Color all of the nouns red. Color all of the pronouns blue. Color all of the verbs green.

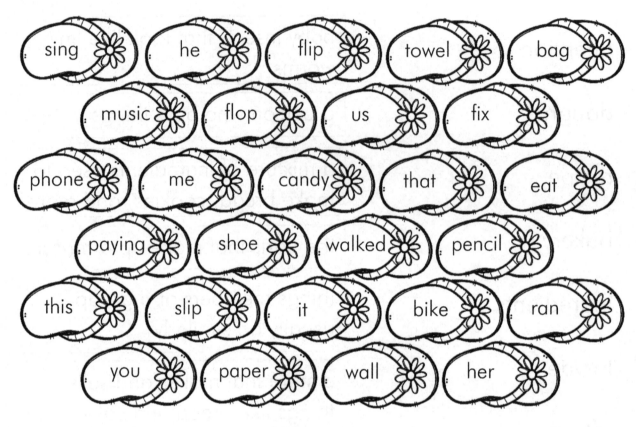

sing   he   flip   towel   bag

music   flop   us   fix

phone   me   candy   that   eat

paying   shoe   walked   pencil

this   slip   it   bike   ran

you   paper   wall   her

Writing

Write a sentence that contains a noun and a verb. Then rewrite the sentence, but replace the noun with a pronoun. If you have more than one noun, see how many you can replace with pronouns.

_____

_____

_____

_____

Writing

Write a story about your vacation to a mountain home (pretend). What did you do there? Was it summer or winter?

_____

_____

_____

_____

_____

_____

_____

_____

_____

_____

Blends

Look at each picture and the choices of blends. Circle the blend that either begins or ends the word.

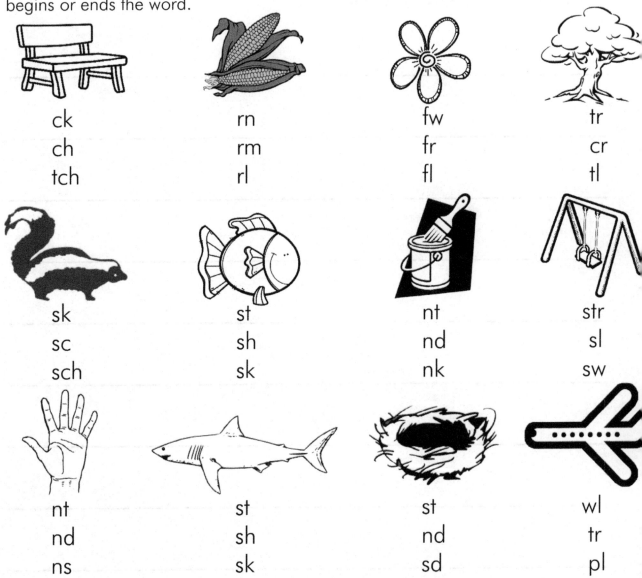

ck
ch
tch

rn
rm
rl

fw
fr
fl

tr
cr
tl

sk
sc
sch

st
sh
sk

nt
nd
nk

str
sl
sw

nt
nd
ns

st
sh
sk

st
nd
sd

wl
tr
pl

Writing

Using your best handwriting, write words that end in **ck**. Write: *brick, trick, click, tick,* and then three other ck words you come up with.

_____

_____

Contractions

Find which tree the contraction apple goes to. Draw a line from the apple to the right tree.

Use the lines below to write the contractions for: *we will, I have, you are, he is,* and two others of your choice.

_____

_____

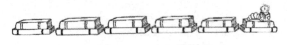

Spelling Suffixes

Using the words in the box, write each word next to its definition. Be sure to write as neatly as you can. Can you figure out what each **suffix** or word ending means based on the common definitions?

bravely   slowly   sadly   cheerful   hopeful
fearless   useless   kindness   loudness

full of cheer _____

without use _____

in a way that is brave _____

being loud _____

in a way that is sad _____

full of hope _____

without fear _____

in a way that is slow _____

being kind _____

Word Builder

Choose the letters from the box that best fit the blanks within the sentences. Write them in your neatest handwriting. Do you hear a common sound in the finished words? Write each completed word on the lines at the bottom of the page.

| og | lo | all | ra | ta | aw |

I needed to c_____ my mom when I was ready to be picked up.

My d_____ is the smartest one on the planet.

I love to d_____w pictures for my dad.

I tripped on a _____g on our hike.

I s_____ a frog on our porch.

My brother is so _____ll he can touch the ceiling.

_____

_____

Writing

Write a story. Start: *He bravely...* or *She bravely...* Then use at least one other word from the word box (from lesson 148). Write at least four sentences. Make sure each of your sentences starts with a capital letter and ends with punctuation.

bravely	slowly	sadly	cheerful	hopeful
fearless	useless	kindness	loudness	

_____

_____

_____

_____

_____

_____

_____

_____

Word Match

Draw a line from the word to its definition. Then write all of the words on the lines at the bottom, using your very best handwriting.

fussed	two feelers on the head of an insect
penalty	helpful or beneficial
grumpily	gave their word that they would do something
groaned	mad
antennae	complained in an angry or disgruntled way
grumbled	punishment for disobeying some sort of rule
promised	protested or complained
advantage	acting in a grumpy way
angry	made a moaning sound

_____

_____

_____

Writing

Copy this sentence: *"I'm afraid I don't know how,"* *replied the country lad.* Pay attention to all of the punctuation and capitalization.

_____

_____

_____

What are the two contractions in the sentence?

_____

What do the contractions mean?

_____

Can you find a pronoun in the sentence?

_____

Can you find a common noun in the sentence?

_____

Writing

Copy this sentence: *"I'll have to teach Danny Rugg a good lesson," said Bert to his cousin.* Pay attention to all of the punctuation and capitalization.

_____

_____

_____

_____

What is the contraction in the sentence?

_____

What does the contraction mean?

_____

Can you find a pronoun in the sentence?

_____

Can you find any proper nouns in the sentence?

_____

Writing

Copy this sentence: *"That's what we'll do!" cried Bert, steering toward it.* Pay attention to all of the punctuation and capitalization.

_____

_____

_____

There is an 's word in the sentence. Is it possessive or a contraction?

_____

What does it mean?

_____

Can you find a pronoun in the sentence?

_____

Can you find a proper noun in the sentence?

_____

Writing

Write sentences like the ones you have been copying. Write what someone is saying and use a contraction. Here are some examples: *"I'll be right there,"* I *said. "He's coming for dinner,"* I told my mom. *"It's time to go!"* I yelled. Write three sentences like the examples.

_____

_____

_____

_____

_____

_____

_____

_____

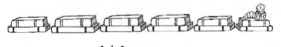

Writing

Copy this sentence: *By this time the snowslide had reached the tree, and the mass was now much larger than at first.* Can you draw a picture of what is happening?

_____

_____

_____

_____

Word Builder

Choose the letters from the box that best fit the blanks within the sentences.
Write them in your neatest handwriting. Write each completed word on the lines
at the bottom of the page.

ew	ot	ok	bl	oo	ou

The wind _____ew so hard it knocked
over my bicycle.

My father's bo_____ was so muddy it
left tracks all over the floor.

The m_____n is full and beautiful tonight.

I got some n_____ shoes yesterday.

It to_____ a week but I finished the
whole book.

I hope y_____ have a great day!

_____

_____

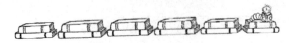

Word Match

Draw a line from the word to its definition. Then write all of the words on the lines at the bottom, using your very best handwriting.

horizon

thunder

delivery

bolt

dispatch

disguise

weather

rumbled

lightning

changing the way you look; looking like someone else

a flash of light during a storm

what it's like outside, including temperature and winds

made a deep rolling sound

bringing something to someone or some place

where the sky and earth appear to meet

to send out

a strike of lightning

noise you hear during a storm

_____

_____

_____

Writing

Copy this sentence: *Then came another thaw, and a freeze followed some days later, making good skating.*

_____

_____

_____

_____

Can you find a plural noun in the sentence?

_____

Can you find the two past tense verbs?

_____

Can you find the present tense verb?

_____

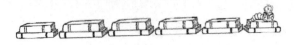

Writing

Think of any place in the world you would like to go. Why would you like to go there? Write about it. Tell where you would like to go and why. What would you do when you got there? How long would you stay?

_____

_____

_____

_____

_____

_____

_____

_____

_____

Vowel Pairing

Use the apples to pick the vowels that are missing from each word. Write them in the blank.

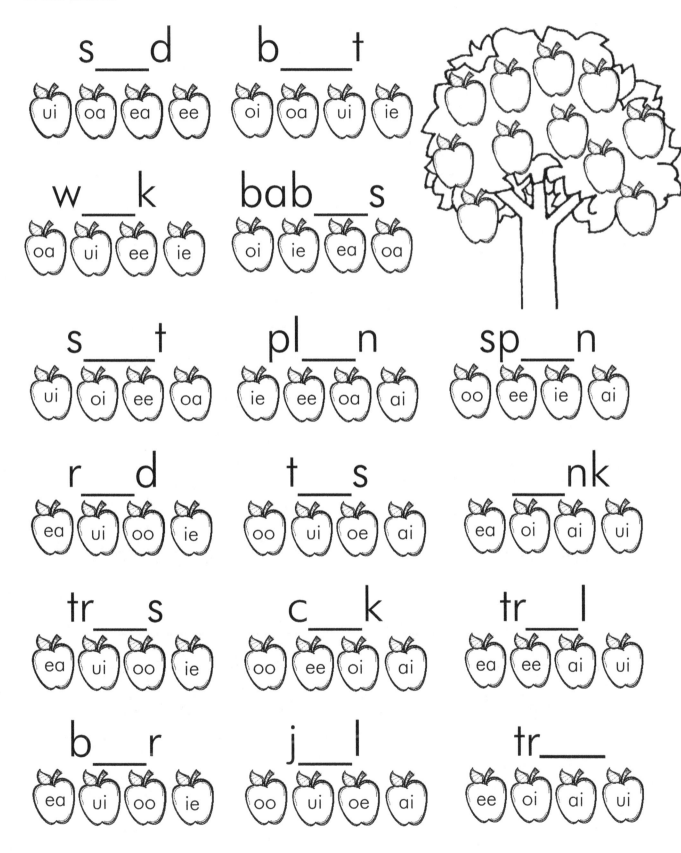

s__d
ui oa ea ee

b___t
oi oa ui ie

w__k
oa ui ee ie

bab__s
oi ie ea oa

s___t
ui oi ee oa

pl__n
ie ee oa ai

sp__n
oo ee ie ai

r__d
ea ui oo ie

t__s
oo ui oe ai

__nk
ea oi ai ui

tr__s
ea ui oo ie

c__k
oo ee oi ai

tr__l
ea ee ai ui

b__r
ea ui oo ie

j__l
oo ui oe ai

tr___
ee oi ai ui

Grammar

Write which of the two underlined words answer the question for each sentence. Be careful! Some of the words can be both nouns and verbs, so the context of the sentence is important to decide which way they are being used.

Which word is the verb?

I practiced my flute.

_____

Which word is the noun?

I went to soccer practice.

_____

Which word is the noun?

The dog barked.

_____

Which word is the verb?

My shoe is untied.

_____

Which word is the verb?

He jumped off the swing.

_____

Which word is the noun?

She swung from the tree.

_____

Which word is the verb?

The ball rolled downhill.

_____

Which word is the verb?

The roll was delicious.

_____

Which word is the noun?

We shopped all day.

_____

Which word is the noun?

The shop felt cold.

_____

Matching

These spelling words sound the same but are spelled differently. Read through the words and simplified definitions first – the definitions are to the right of the words. Then cut them out and mix them up. Play a matching game to help you learn which spelling word goes with which definition.

see	look at	sea	the ocean
deer	the animal	dear	beloved one
die	stop living	dye	a coloring
meet	come together	meat	the food
road	a street	rode	travelled on or in

(This page left intentionally blank)

Spelling

Do you remember your spelling words? See if you can write the correct word beside each simplified definition from lesson 163.

_____ look at

_____ the ocean

_____ the animal

_____ beloved one

_____ stop living

_____ a coloring

_____ come together

_____ the food

_____ a street

_____ travelled on or in

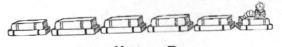

Language Arts
Level 2

Lesson
165

Spelling Bee

Using your same words from the last two lessons, fill in the blanks below. If you need to check on a word or definition, you can use lesson 163 to help you.

I _____ blue skies today.

The _____ is salty.

A _____ came into our yard last night.

My family is very _____ to me.

The leaves _____ and fall in autumn.

We used green _____ on our project.

Can we _____ at the park?

Vegetarians don't eat _____.

The _____ was full of traffic.

We _____ our bikes all weekend.

Final Research Project

Choose the topic for your final research project. It can be an animal, a person, a place, an invention – anything you want. Write the title of your project on the line and then draw a picture like this is the cover of a book you are making. Write your name on the line at the bottom as the author.

_____

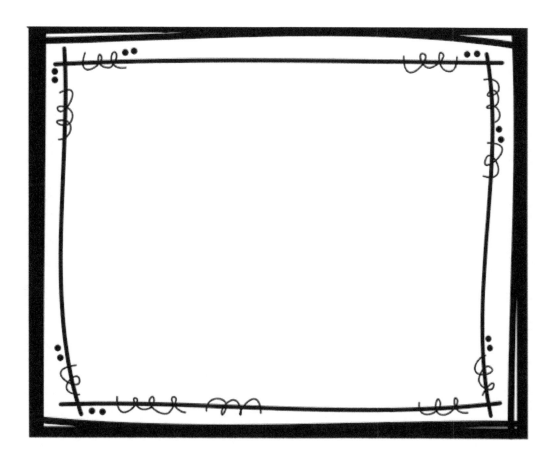

_____

(This page left intentionally blank)

Final Research Project

Do research on your topic. Look in books you have or search online if you are allowed. When you find something interesting, write it down. Do not copy word for word what you read; make the words your own. Be sure to write at the bottom where you found your information or the **resources** you used.

_____

_____

_____

_____

_____

_____

Resources: _____

_____

_____

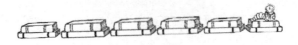

Final Research Project

Do research on your topic. Look in books you have or search online if you are allowed. When you find something interesting, write it down. Do not copy word for word what you read; make the words your own. Be sure to write at the bottom where you found your information or the **resources** you used.

_____

_____

_____

_____

_____

_____

Resources:_____

_____

_____

Final Research Project

Do research on your topic. Look in books you have or search online if you are allowed. When you find something interesting, write it down. Do not copy word for word what you read; make the words your own. Be sure to write at the bottom where you found your information or the **resources** you used.

_____

_____

_____

_____

_____

_____

Resources:_____

_____

_____

(This page left intentionally blank)

Final Research Project

Now use your information to write sentences. Each page of your book should have a fact that you learned. Try to draw a picture about it as well. Use proper capitalization and punctuation in your sentences.

_____

_____

_____

_____

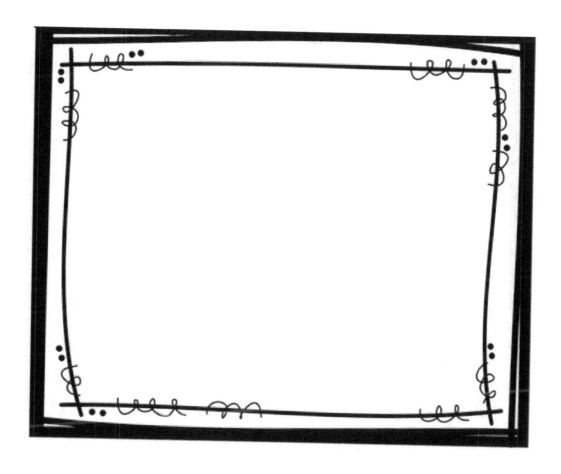

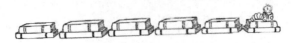

Final Research Project

Write a new sentence telling a new fact. Try to draw a picture about it as well. Use proper capitalization and punctuation in your sentence.

_____

_____

_____

_____

Final Research Project

Write a new sentence telling a new fact. Try to draw a picture about it as well.
Use proper capitalization and punctuation in your sentence.

_____

_____

_____

_____

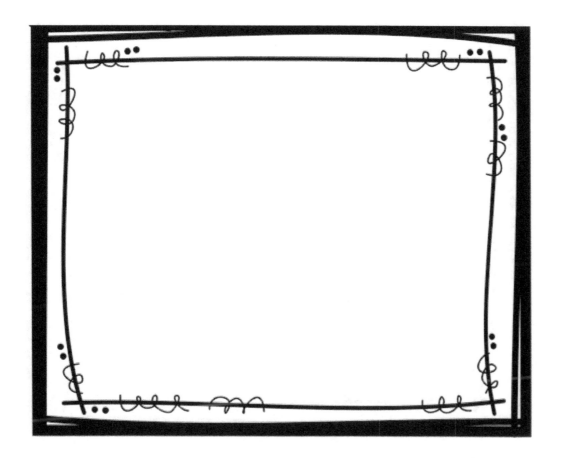

Final Research Project

Write a new sentence telling a new fact. Try to draw a picture about it as well. Use proper capitalization and punctuation in your sentence.

_____

_____

_____

_____

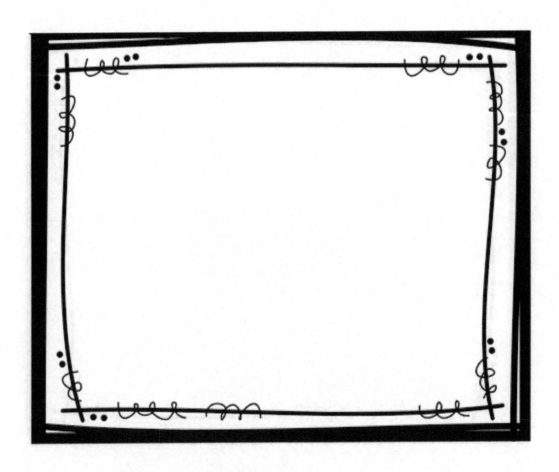

Final Research Project

Write a new sentence telling a new fact. Try to draw a picture about it as well. Use proper capitalization and punctuation in your sentence.

_____

_____

_____

_____

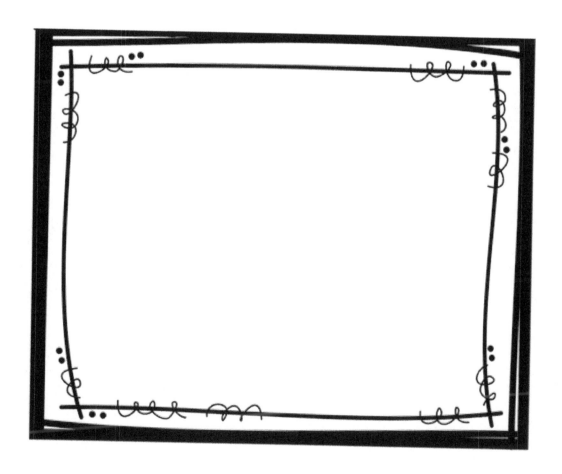

(This page left intentionally blank)

Final Research Project

Compile all of your resources information from your notes from lessons 167-169 onto this page so they're all in one place. Line them up neatly on the page.

_____

_____

_____

_____

_____

_____

_____

_____

(This page left intentionally blank)

Final Research Project

Write the first page of your book. Write one sentence that tells what you learned about. This will be the **introduction** to your book. Draw a picture.

_____

_____

_____

_____

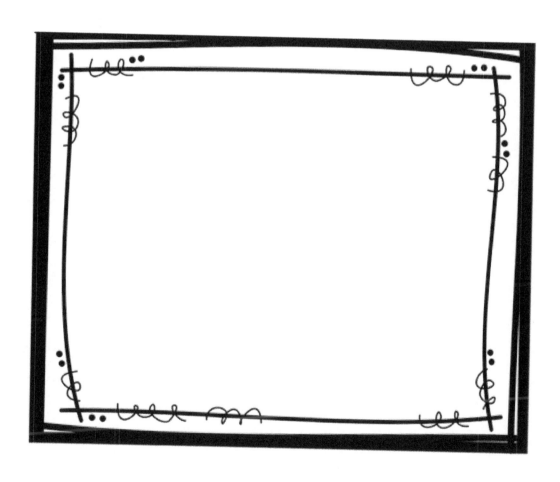

(This page left intentionally blank)

Final Research Project

Write the last page of your book. Tell what you think about the topic you studied. This will be the **conclusion** to your book.

_____

_____

_____

_____

_____

_____

(This page left intentionally blank)

Final Research Project

If you want to assemble your book in order by removing the pages from this workbook, this is the order they should go in: lesson 166, lesson 176, lessons 170-174, lesson 177, lesson 175. (Most professional authors don't write their books in order either!) As you compile it, make sure there are no mistakes. Show it to someone and be proud of your work!

Practice your editing skills. Circle what's wrong in the sentences below.

uncle phil is a really good dancer.

My mom likes to feed the dear in our backyard.

my brothers favorite sport is hockey.

The three girl's dresses all matched.

The foxs went to their den for some rest

our coach stayd with us while we waited for are parents.

The boys went home, but i helped dad finish his work?

Watch out. The stove is very hot.

Final Research Project

Now write your book all as one paragraph on the lines below.

Verb Review

Let's review verbs one last time! Color all of the linking verbs blue. Color all of the action verbs green. All of the flowers should be colored when you are done.

Congratulations!

You have finished Language Arts 2!

The Easy Peasy All-in-One Homeschool is a free, complete online homeschool curriculum. There are 180 days of ready-to-go assignments for every level and every subject. It's created for your children to work as independently as you want them to. Preschool through high school is available as well as courses ranging from English, math, science and history to art, music, computer, thinking, physical education and health. A daily Bible lesson is offered as well. The mission of Easy Peasy is to enable those to homeschool who otherwise thought they couldn't.

The Genesis Curriculum takes the Bible and turns it into lessons for your homeschool. Daily lessons include Bible reading, memory verse, spelling, handwriting, vocabulary, grammar, Biblical language, science, social studies, writing, and thinking through discussion questions.

The Genesis Curriculum uses a complete book of the Bible for one full year. The curriculum is being made using both Old and New Testament books. Find us online at genesiscurriculum.com to read about the latest developments in this expanding curriculum.

Made in the USA
Las Vegas, NV
15 August 2021

28015513R00116